SMALL GROUP SERIES

Parenting

Raising Faithful Younger Adolescents

Augsburg Fortress, Minneapolis

Contents

INTERSECTIONS
Small Group Series

Parenting
Raising Faithful Younger Adolescents

Developed in cooperation with the Division for Congregational Ministries

George S. Johnson, series introduction
John Roberto, Center for Ministry Development editor
Contributor: Janet Drey
Editors: Laurie J. Hanson and Elizabeth Drotning
The Wells Group, series design
Cover photo: © 2001 PhotoDisc
Page 13, 19, 39 photos: © 2001 PhotoDisc
Page 45 photo: © 2001 EyeWire
Page 21 illustration: Brian Jensen/Studio Arts

Materials identified as *LBW* are from *Lutheran Book of Worship*, copyright 1978.

Scripture quotations are from New Revised Standard Version Bible, copyright 1989 Division of Christian
Education of the National Council of the Churches of Christ in the United States of America. Used by permission.

Copyright © 2001 Augsburg Fortress
All rights reserved. May not be reproduced.
ISBN 0-8066-4197-5
Manufactured in U.S.A.

Introduction

A quick look at the family section of your local bookstore will reveal dozens of books about parenting. What you probably will not find among these titles is a book about parenting and faith growth. *Raising Faithful Younger Adolescents* is specifically designed for parents who have sons and daughters 10-14 years of age. This study provides an understanding of the unique characteristics of younger adolescents and ideas and strategies for nurturing faith in their lives by sharing gospel values, celebrating rituals, praying together, serving those in need, and developing a strong family life. *Raising Faithful Younger Adolescents* also suggests ways that you also can continue growing as you walk with your son or daughter in faith.

This study provides you with an understanding of the unique characteristics of younger adolescents and their families. Younger adolescents are caught up in the challenges presented by puberty, new ways of thinking, an expanded circle of contacts and friends, growing autonomy, and the need to redefine family relationships. But they still need your concern and care.

You can continue to influence your son or daughter's faith and values, and grow with them in the process! This book and your small group can give you and your family support and encouragement for raising a faithful younger adolescent.

Developmental assets

Search Institute, a research and educational organization in Minneapolis, has compiled a list of 40 developmental assets for younger adolescents. (See page 52.) These assets are components identified in the lives of healthy, happy, well-adjusted young adolescents. They are named in this course as an awareness-raising guide as we work to raise healthy, faithful adolescents.

Baptismal promises

This baptismal symbol appears in each chapter next to activities that remind us of the promises we make when our children are baptized.

SMALL GROUP SERIES

Welcome into the family of those who are part of small groups! Intersections Small Group Series will help you and other members of your group build relationships and discover ways to connect the Christian faith with your everyday life.

This book is prepared for those who want to make a difference in this world, who want to grow in their Christian faith, as well as for those who are beginning to explore the Christian faith. The information in this introduction to the Intersections small group experience can help your group make the most out of your time together.

Biblical encouragement

Do not be conformed to this world, but be transformed by the renewing of your minds, so that you may discern what is the will of God—what is good and acceptable and perfect. Romans 12:2.

Small groups provide an atmosphere where the Holy Spirit can transform lives. As you share your life stories and learn together, God's Spirit can work to enlighten and direct you.

Strength is provided to face the pressures to conform to forces and influences that are opposed to what is "good and acceptable and perfect." To "be transformed" is an ongoing experience of God's grace as we take up the cross and follow Jesus. Changed lives happen as we live in community with one another. Small groups encourage such change and growth.

What is a small group?

A number of definitions and descriptions of the small group ministry experience exist throughout the church. Roberta Hestenes, a Presbyterian pastor and author, defines a small group as an intentional face-to-face gathering of three to twelve people who meet regularly with the common purpose of discovering and growing in the possibilities of the abundant life.

Whatever definition you use, the following characteristics are important.

Small—Seven to ten people is ideal so that everyone can be heard and no one's voice is lost. More than twelve members makes genuine caring difficult.

Intentional—Commitment to the group is a high priority.

Personal—Sharing experiences and insights is more important than mastering content.

Conversational—Leaders that facilitate conversation, rather than teach, are the key to encouraging participation.

Friendly—Having a warm, accepting, nonjudgmental atmosphere is essential.

Christ-centered—The small-group experience is biblically based, related to the real world, and founded on Christ.

Features of Intersections Small Group Series

A small-group model

A number of small-group ministry models exist. Most models include three types of small groups:

- *Discipleship groups*—where people gather to grow in Christian faith and life;

- *Support and recovery groups*—which focus on special interests, concerns, or needs; and

- *Ministry groups*—which have a task-oriented focus.

Intersections Small Group Series offers material for all of these.

For discipleship groups, this series offers a variety of courses with Bible study at the center. What makes a discipleship group different from traditional group Bible studies? In discipleship groups, members bring their life experience to the exploration of the biblical material.

For support and recovery groups, Intersections Small Group Series offers topical material to assist group members in dealing with issues related to their common experience, hurt, or interest. An extra section of facilitator helps in the back of the book will assist leaders of support and recovery groups to anticipate and prepare for special circumstances and needs that may arise as group members explore a topic.

Ministry groups can benefit from an environment that includes prayer, biblical reflection, and relationship building, in addition to their task focus.

Four essentials

Prayer, personal sharing, biblical reflection, and a group ministry task are part of each time you gather. These are all important for Christian community to be experienced. Each of the six chapter themes in each book includes:

- Short prayers to open and close your time together.

- Carefully worded questions to make personal sharing safe, nonthreatening, and voluntary.

- A biblical base from which to understand and discover the power and grace of God. God's Word is the compass that keeps the group on course.

- A group ministry task to encourage both individuals and the group as a whole to find ways to put faith into action.

Flexibility

Each book contains six chapter themes that may be covered in six sessions or easily extended for groups that meet for a longer period of time. Each chapter theme is organized around two to three main topics with supplemental material to make it easily adaptable to your small group's needs. You need not use all the material. Most themes will work well for 1½- to 2-hour sessions, but a variety of scheduling options is possible.

Bible-based

Each of the six chapter themes in the book includes one or more Bible texts printed in its entirety from the New Revised Standard Version of the Bible. This makes it easy for all group members to read and learn from the same text. Participants will be encouraged through questions, with exercises, and by other group members to address biblical texts in the context of their own lives.

User-friendly

The material is prepared in such a way that it is easy to follow, practical, and does not require a professional to lead it. Designating one to be the facilitator to guide the group is important, but there is no requirement for this person to be theologically trained or an expert in the course topic. Many times options are given so that no one will feel forced into any set way of responding.

Group goals and process

1. **Creating a group covenant or contract for your time together will be important.** During your first meeting, discuss these important characteristics of all small groups and decide how your group will handle them.

Confidentiality—Agreeing that sensitive issues that are shared remain in the group.

Regular attendance—Agreeing to make meetings a top priority.

Nonjudgmental behavior—Agreeing to confess one's own shortcomings, if appropriate, not those of others, and not giving advice unless asked for it.

Prayer and support—Being sensitive to one another, listening, becoming a caring community.

Accountability—Being responsible to each other and open to change.

Items in your covenant should be agreed upon by all members. Add to the group covenant as you go along. Space to record key aspects is included in the back of this book. See page 51.

2. **Everyone is responsible for the success of the group, but do arrange to have one facilitator who can guide the group process each time you meet.**

The facilitator is not a teacher or healer. Teaching, learning, and healing happen from the group experience. The facilitator is more of a shepherd who leads the flock to where they can feed and drink and feel safe.

Remember, an important goal is to experience genuine love and community in a Christ-centered atmosphere. To help make this happen, the facilitator encourages active listening and honest sharing. This person allows the material to facilitate opportunities for self-awareness and interaction with others.

Leadership is shared in a healthy group, but the facilitator is the one designated to set the pace, keep the group focused, and enable the members to support and care for each other.

People need to sense trust and freedom as the group develops; therefore, avoid "shoulds" or "musts" in your group.

3. **Taking on a group ministry task can help members of your group balance personal growth with service to others.**

In your first session, identify ways your group can offer help to others within the congregation or in your surrounding community. Take time at each meeting to do or arrange for that ministry task. Many times it is in the doing that we discover what we believe or how God is working in our lives.

4. **Starting or continuing a personal action plan offers a way to address personal needs that you become aware of in your small-group experience.**

For example, you might want to spend more time in conversation with a friend or spouse. Your action plan might state, "I plan to visit with Terry two times before our next small-group meeting."

If you decide to pursue a personal action plan, consider sharing it with your small group. Your group can be helpful in at least three ways: by giving support; helping to define the plan in realistic, measurable ways; and offering a source to whom you can be accountable.

5. **Prayer is part of small-group fellowship.** There is great power in group prayer, but not everyone feels free to offer spontaneous prayer. That's okay.

Learning to pray aloud takes time and practice. If you feel uncomfortable, start with simple and short prayers. And remember to pray for other members between sessions.

Use page 51 in the back of this book to note prayer requests made by group members.

6. Consider using a journal to help reflect on your experiences and insights between meeting times.

Writing about feelings, ideas, and questions can be one way to express yourself; plus it helps you remember what so often gets lost with time.

The "Daily Walk" component includes material that can get your journaling started. This, of course, is up to you and need not be done on any regular schedule. Even doing it once a week can be time well spent.

How to use this book

The material provided for each session is organized around some key components. If you are the facilitator for your small group, be sure to read this section carefully.

The facilitator's role is to establish a hospitable atmosphere and set a tone that encourages participants to share, reflect, and listen to each other. Some important practical things can help make this happen.

- Whenever possible meet in homes. Be sure to provide clear directions about how to get there.

- Use name tags for several sessions.

- Place the chairs in a circle and close enough for everyone to hear and feel connected.

- Be sure everyone has access to a book; preparation will pay off.

- Have Bibles available and encourage participants to bring their own.

Welcoming

In this study, parents and guardians of younger adolescents can come together to explore how to nurture faith in their families and in the lives of their teenagers. This study provides a balance between understanding the faith of younger adolescents and developing practical ideas and strategies to nurture faith at home. Encourage parents to practice these ideas and strategies at home between group sessions. In your small group, parents and guardians of younger adolescents can receive encouragement and support for their efforts to build a family of faith.

Make necessary arrangements so that the physical and emotional environment for this group is as relaxed and comfortable as possible. Encourage people to come as they are, whether in business suits or gardening clothes. Make arrangements for child-care options to be available. Seek volunteer caregivers or shared child-care opportunities so that financial constraints do not keep people from attending.

Create a cozy atmosphere. Comfortable seating and space where everyone can converse with one another and be part of the group is vital. Encourage people to bring photos of their children to share with the group.

Focus

Each of the six chapter themes in this book has a brief focus statement. Read it aloud. It will give everyone a sense of the direction for each session and provide some boundaries so that people will not feel lost or frustrated trying to cover everything. The focus also connects the theme to the course topic.

Community building

This opening activity is crucial to a relaxed, friendly atmosphere. It will prepare the ground for gradual group development. Two "Community Building" options are provided under each theme. With the facilitator giving his or her response to the questions first, others are free to follow.

One purpose for this section is to allow everyone to participate as he or she responds to nonthreatening questions. The activity serves as a check-in time when participants are invited to share how things are going or what is new.

Make this time light and fun; remember, humor is a welcome gift. Use fifteen to twenty minutes for this activity in your first few sessions and keep the entire group together.

During your first meeting, encourage group members to write down names and phone numbers (when appropriate) of the other members, so people can keep in touch. Use page 50 for this purpose.

Discovery

This component focuses on exploring the theme for your time together, using material that is read and questions and exercises that encourage sharing of personal insights and experiences.

Reading material includes a Bible text with supplemental passages and commentary written by the topic writer. Have volunteers read the Bible texts aloud. The main passage to be used is printed so that everyone operates from a common translation and sees the text.

"A Further Look" is included in some places to give you additional study material if time permits. Use it to explore related passages and questions. Be sure to have extra Bibles handy.

Questions and exercises related to the theme will invite personal sharing and storytelling. Keep in mind that as you listen to each other's stories, you are inspired to live more fully in the grace and will of God. Such exchanges make Christianity relevant and transformation more likely to happen. Caring relationships are key to clarifying one's beliefs. Sharing personal experiences and insights is what makes the small group spiritually satisfying.

Most people are open to sharing their life stories, especially if they're given permission to do so and they know someone will actively listen. Starting with the facilitator's response usually works best. On some occasions you may want to break the group into units of three or four persons to explore certain questions. When you reconvene, relate your experience to the whole group. Appoint someone to start the discussion.

Wrap-up

Plan your schedule so that there will be enough time for wrapping up. This time can include work on your group ministry task, review of key discoveries during your time together, identifying personal and prayer concerns, closing prayers, and the Lord's Prayer.

The facilitator can help the group identify and plan its ministry task. Introduce the idea and decide on your group ministry task in the first session. Tasks need not be grandiose. Activities might include:

- Ministry in your community, such as adopting a food shelf, clothes closet, or homeless shelter; sponsoring equipment, food, or clothing drives; or sending members to staff the shelter.

- Ministry to members of the congregation, such as writing notes to those who are ill or bereaved.

- Congregational tasks where volunteers are always needed, such as serving refreshments during the fellowship time after worship, stuffing envelopes for a church mailing, or taking responsibility for altar preparations for one month.

Depending upon the task, you can use part of each meeting time to carry out or plan the task.

In the "Wrap-up," allow time for people to share insights and encouragement and to voice special prayer requests. Just to mention someone who needs prayer is a form of prayer. The "Wrap-up" time may include a brief worship experience with candles, prayers, and singing. You might form a circle and hold hands. Silence can be effective. If you use the Lord's Prayer in your group, select the version that is known in your setting. There is space on page 50 to record the version your group uses. Another closing prayer is also printed on page 50. Before you go, ask members to pray for one another during the week. Remember also any special concerns or prayer requests.

Daily walk

Seven Bible readings and a verse, thought, and prayer for the journey related to the material just discussed are provided for those who want to keep the theme before them between sessions. These brief readings may be used for devotional time. Some group members may want to memorize selected passages. The Bible readings also can be used for supplemental study by the group if needed. Prayer for other group members also can be part of this time of personal reflection.

A word of encouragement

No material is ever complete or perfect for every situation or group. Creativity and imagination will be important gifts for the facilitator to bring to each theme. Keep in mind that it is in community that we are challenged to grow in Jesus Christ. Together we become what we could not become alone. It is God's plan that it be so.

For additional resources and ideas see *Starting Small Groups—and Keeping Them Going* (Minneapolis: Augsburg Fortress, 1995).

1 Nurturing the Growth of Younger Adolescents

Focus

Adolescence is a time of rapid change for the young person as well as the family, which presents parents with new challenges and opportunities for nurturing faith growth.

Community building

Option

Think about your family, what it is like now and what it was like when your younger adolescent was a grade-schooler. How have things changed? How have they stayed the same? (Think about the people in your family, your home, family activities, and so forth.)

Introduce yourselves to one another. Share your children's names and their ages. Share responses to the six unfinished sentences with each other.

- One of the best things about being a parent of a younger adolescent is…

- One of the most challenging things about being a parent of a younger adolescent is…

- One thing I've learned from my son/daughter is…

- One thing I still need to learn as a parent of a younger adolescent is…

- The biggest change in my parenting style is…

- As a parent, one thing I am afraid of is…

Read the prayer together.

Opening prayer

Loving God, thank you for the gift of our young people. Give us the insight and wisdom to understand them at this new stage in life, to accept the changes that are unfolding in their lives, and to embrace the new opportunities and challenges we face as parents. Amen

Read and discuss.

The growing young adolescent

Adolescence is a time of change and challenge, but almost all young people—and their parents—survive it without serious problems. If young people feel good about their family life, everything else about being an adolescent will be a little bit easier. For parents, adolescence can be much more than a time of "problems"—it can be a time of great pride as sons and daughters grow in their new abilities, independent thinking, and sense of self.

- Identify several changes that are happening in the life of your younger adolescent right now.

A time of change

Consider the remarkable and significant changes that younger adolescents experience:

Younger adolescents are experiencing tremendous physical and sexual development as they grow into their adult bodies. Not only are young adolescents sensitive about this, these bodily changes impact their self-esteem and self-image.

Younger adolescents gradually develop the ability to think abstractly, idealistically, logically, and reflectively. As they work at defining themselves, younger adolescents become self-conscious, critical, and self-centered, and challenge and question rules, limits, and parental values.

Younger adolescents enter a broader social world consisting of parents, peer groups, and activity groups. In general, younger adolescents look to their parents for affection, values, acceptance, and guidance, especially about the future. They look to their peers on issues of style (music, dress) and social life (choice of friends and activities) and are susceptible to pressure from peers to conform.

Younger adolescents seek limited independence and autonomy from parents and adults. They want and need to take charge of their own lives, make their own decisions, choose their own friends, plan their own activities, think their own thoughts, and dream their own dreams. The relationship between parent and child inevitably changes as the adolescent becomes less an extension of the family and more an individual.

Younger adolescents engage in more complex moral decision-making. They tend to make moral judgments based on what is expected of them by family, peers, and other persons significant in their lives. They are developing the ability to empathize with others, but need help in developing a strong set of moral values and the courage to stand up for what they believe is right.

Younger adolescents are seeking to discover who they are as people of faith. They can develop the beliefs, values, and practices of the Christian faith from their family and from active involvement in the life of a faith community. They seek realistic role models of faith; occasions to share faith stories; experiences of the Christian faith—worship, service, prayer, leadership; and opportunities to explore the roots of the Christian life in Scripture and church teachings.

- Does this list of characteristics describe what your son or daughter is experiencing? If so, in what ways?

- How might understanding the characteristics of younger adolescents help you become a more effective parent?

Discovery

Have someone read the Scripture passage aloud.

Luke 6:47-49

[47] "I will show you what someone is like who comes to me, hears my words, and acts on them. [48] That one is like a man building a house, who dug deeply and laid the foundation on rock; when a flood arose, the river burst against that house but could not shake it, because it had been well built. [49] But the one who hears and does not act is like a man who built a house on the ground without a foundation. When the river burst against it, immediately it fell, and great was the ruin of that house."

Developing a family that promotes growth

Forty developmental assets identified by the Search Institute provide the building blocks that help adolescents grow up to be healthy, well- adjusted, and strong. Just as immunizations keep young people healthy and protect them from disease, these 40 assets help adolescents make healthy choices and inoculate them against a wide range of risk-taking behaviors. The more assets young people have, the more likely they are to be healthy and engage in positive behaviors. These 40 developmental assets have been divided into eight categories:

a. Support
b. Empowerment
c. Boundaries and Expectations
d. Constructive Use of Time
e. Commitment to Learning
f. Positive Values
g. Social Competencies
h. Positive Identity

Turn to the list of assets on pages 52-53. Form teams and divide up the eight categories.

Consider this

The asset-building approach gives a concrete, sensible perspective for thinking about parenting and family life. Parents can promote healthy growth in their younger adolescents' lives and must stay involved even though young people seek more and more independence.

Together with your team, review the assets in your category and suggest ways in which families with younger adolescents can put these assets into practice.

■ How important are these assets for nurturing the growth of younger adolescents?

■ What can parents do to promote these assets?

■ How can you strengthen your practice of these assets in your family?

Form groups of three to discuss the questions, then discuss responses as a large group.

Group goals and ministry tasks

Read about group goals and group ministry tasks on pages 6-7 in this book.

■ What do you hope to accomplish in this small-group course?

■ Brainstorm group ministry task ideas that include the younger adolescents in your families.

■ Bring your ideas to the whole group for discussion and

decision-making.

Reaching out in Christ's love is a powerful way to learn. Consider projects aimed at the needs of younger adolescents, such as after-school programs, tutoring or literacy programs, and mentoring programs for young people. Record your goals and group ministry task in the appendix on page 51.

Discovery

■ What do you consider the essentials that every younger adolescent needs from his or her parents?

What every younger adolescent needs from a parent

Throughout their book, *10 Best Gifts for Your Teen* (Notre Dame, IN: Ave Maria Press, 1999), Patt and Steve Saso identify what young people need from parents.

Respect: Respect is the key to successful parenting at this stage. Respecting adolescents means to look at what they are going through, take them seriously, separate what they do from who they are, avoid comparisons, and honor their plans.

Room: Giving your son or daughter room means allowing them to keep their bedroom in a way that reflects their personality and providing the privacy they need to begin the process of becoming their own person.

Receptivity: To be receptive to what your adolescent is saying, stop what you are doing, face him or her, make eye contact, and listen with your full attention.

Revelation of self: Share about your past and your present, as well as your dreams for the future. When you share your very human struggles and reflect on your life experiences, you are inviting your son or daughter to do the same.

Responsibility: Nurture responsible behavior in your son or daughter by giving them choices and holding them accountable for the consequences, helping them set goals, giving them responsibilities at home, holding regular family meetings, and modeling responsible behavior.

Resolve: Parenting with resolve includes sharing and living out your values, setting clear limits and rules to keep your son or daughter safe, using natural and logical consequences, being consistent and following through when those limits or rules are broken, using mistakes as an opportunity to learn, and building a family support system with other families in the congregation and community.

Recognition: Recognition means honoring your adolescent for their successes, hard work, and strengths. Give recognition to your adolescent by affirming positive behavior and personal qualities, expressing love and saying "I love you," trusting them, attending their events, and accepting them.

Reconciliation: Everyone makes mistakes. By admitting your mistakes and seeking forgiveness with your adolescent, you heal a wounded relationship, model the ability to admit mistakes and seek forgiveness, and offer them the opportunity to extend forgiveness. As a result, your son or daughter will be more open to admitting their mistakes and seeking forgiveness.

Release: Release is the gift of "letting go," giving your adolescent more and more freedom as they get older, encouraging them to be their own person, and helping them to grow up.

Role-modeling: As parents, we need to model the very behaviors we want to see in our adolescents as they grow into adults.

■ What new ideas did you discover? What would you add to your list of essentials?

■ Which of these ideas can you start working on right now? How will you start?

See the resource list on page 54 for more information on parenting younger adolescents.

A further look

Read the paragraph silently and write down responses to the questions, then discuss your responses as a group.

A parent's baptismal promise

At baptism parents promise to train their children in the practice of the Christian faith and to bring up their children to keep God's commandments by loving God and neighbor.

Take a few minutes now or during the week to consider what you want for your young person now and in the future. Write down your ideas if you wish.

■ How will you define success as a parent? What will you need to do in order to be a successful parent?

■ What role would you like faith to play in your son or daughter's life now and in the future?

Wrap-up

See page 9 in the intro-
duction for a description
of "Wrap-up."

Before you go, take time for the following:

■ Group ministry task

■ Review

■ Personal concerns and prayer concerns

■ Closing prayers

See page 50 for sug-
gested closing prayers.
Page 51 can also be
used for listing ongoing
prayer requests.

Daily walk

Bible readings

Day 1
Matthew 22:34-40

Day 2
John 15:12-17

Day 3
Matthew 5:21-26 and
7:1-5

Day 4
1 Corinthians 13:1-8

Day 5
Colossians 3:12-17

Day 6
Romans 12:9-18

Day 7
1 John 4:7-21

Verse for the journey

If then there is any encouragement in Christ, any consolation
from love, any sharing in the Spirit, any compassion and sym-
pathy, make my joy complete: be of the same mind, having
the same love, being in full accord and of one mind.
Philippians 2:1-2

Thought for the journey

"Parenting is like gardening. By cultivating the soil of your relationship with your teenager—by adding more of the nutri-
ents of love and care, the pruning of a structured environment,
and the sunlight of a positive role model—you will experience
a fruitful harvest."

(Patt and Steve Saso. *10 Best Gifts for Your Teen*.
Notre Dame, IN: Ave Maria Press, 1999, page 136)

Prayer for the journey

God, give us the power to love. Help us to put love at the center of our family's life and make it the focus of our energies.
May we grow more in love with you each day. Amen

2 Sharing Christian Faith and Values

Focus

The family is the primary context for faith growth and values formation. The Christian faith and value system are sources of strength for younger adolescents as they develop their own faith life as followers of Jesus Christ.

Community building

Have paper and pencils or pens available. Take time to reflect on the questions, then share your responses.

Option

Imagine that you are moving and can only take five of your most important possessions. What would you take? (Your children and pets are already safely moved.) Why? What does this say about your values? What items would your younger adolescent take? Why? What does this say about his or her values?

Values are the internal compasses that guide us as we make decisions and set priorities. Many value systems are competing for our attention and loyalty, so we need to be intentional about sharing positive, healthy values with younger adolescents. In this chapter, you will reflect on the values you want to share with your son or daughter and look at several ways you can do this.

Values worth sharing

Values I learned at home: List several values you learned at home when you were growing up.

Values we share: Identify the values you want to share with your son or daughter. Place a check mark next to the values you feel are real strengths in your family today.

Values we want to share: Place a star next to values you want to share with your son or daughter, but feel you are not sharing today.

Opening prayer

Listen, my people, mark each word. I begin with a story, I speak of mysteries welling up from ancient depths. We must not hide this story from our children but tell the mighty works and all the wonders of God.

(Psalm 78:1-4 adapted)

Value voices

Identify values young people are exposed to on a daily basis.

Think about the values younger adolescents are exposed to each day through the following "voices." What are young people seeing and hearing? Give examples. What values are being shared?

      a. Music
      b. TV shows
      c. Commercials and advertisements
      d. Movies
      e. School
      f. Peer groups
      g. Activity groups

■ Which of these "voices" is strongest in the lives of young people? How does your son or daughter decide which "voices" to listen to?

Values for living

Have Bibles available for this activity. Invite each person in the group read one gospel value and the accompanying Gospel passage.

In the gospels, Jesus provides us with essential values for living as a Christian in today's world. Learn more about gospel values in the following Scripture passages.

The call to love one another: John 13:34-35. (See also Matthew 22:34-40, Mark 12:28-34, and Luke 10:25-37.)

The call to love even our enemies and renounce revenge: Luke 6:27-36. (See also Matthew 5:38-48.)

The call to forgive one another and always seek reconciliation: Matthew 5:23-24. (See also Matthew 6:12-15 and 18:21-22.)

The call to avoid judging and condemning others: Luke 6:37-42. (See also Matthew 7:1-6 and John 8:1-11.)

The call to avoid self-righteousness and hypocrisy: Luke 18:9-14. (See also Matthew 6:2-4 and 23:1-31).

The call to befriend those whom society looks down upon: Mark 2:13-17. (See also Luke 8:26-39 and 14:12-24.)

The call to serve one another, humbly and unselfishly: John 13:1-17. (See also Luke 22:24-27.)

The call to serve the poor: Matthew 25:31-40. (See also Luke 16:19-31.)

The corresponding call to beware of riches and attachment to possessions: Luke 12:16-21. (See also Mark 10:17-31, Matthew 6:24-34 and 19:16-30, Luke 16:19-31 and 18:18-29.)

The call to be just in our dealings with others: Matthew 23:1-5 and 23-24.

The call to pray always and with complete trust in God: Luke 11:1-13. (See also Matthew 6:5-15 and 7:7-11.)

Discuss how to apply gospel values as individuals and families.

■ What are some of the challenges of living gospel values in our families and in the world today?

■ What would have to change in your life to live out gospel values more fully?

■ How do gospel values challenge the values young people are exposed to in our society?

■ How can you strengthen the ways you share gospel values with your younger adolescent?

Consider this

Review the six positive values and discuss the questions.

The thoughts and actions of younger adolescents are based on their values—even if these values aren't yet fully developed. When young people have positive values, they grow into caring adults who set high standards for themselves and the people around them.

Search Institute has identified six positive values that are essential for healthy growth: caring, equality and social justice, integrity, honesty, responsibility, and healthy lifestyle. Turn to page 53 to read descriptions of each value.

■ **Why are these values so important for healthy, positive growth?**

■ **How do these values connect with gospel values?**

Deuteronomy 11:1,18-21

Have one person read
the Scripture passage
aloud. Then discuss the
questions.

1 You shall love the Lord your God, therefore, and keep his charge, his decrees, his ordinances, and his commandments always... 18 You shall put these words of mine in your heart and soul, and you shall bind them as a sign on your hand, and fix them as an emblem on your forehead. 19 Teach them to your children, talking about them when you are at home and when you are away, when you lie down and when you rise. 20 Write them on the doorposts of your house and on your gates, 21 so that your days and the days of your children may be multiplied in the land.

- What are several ways you share and live gospel values at home with your younger adolescent?

- What are some of the obstacles that hinder your efforts to teach values?

Sharing values with younger adolescents

Review and discuss.

Parents communicate values to younger adolescents in several different ways:

Congenial or close relationships: Values can be communicated even without words if there is a climate of love and genuine caring. The young person senses the values of the parent and unconsciously internalizes them.

Modeling: Values are modeled in your actions, your use of time, your conversations, and the commitments you make. These values-in-action are the ones your son or daughter will see and imitate.

Personal witness: Communicate values verbally by explaining why a certain issue or value is important to you. Communicate values through the written word by exploring biblical teachings and stories, as well as the lives of people in the Bible. Explore stories of Christian people, from yesterday and today, who have made following Jesus and living the Gospel the top priority in their lives.

Gentle reasoning: Young people are more likely to internalize values if you discuss the positive aspects of a value and the consequences of not living it out (possibly violating their own needs or bringing unhappiness to someone else).

See the resource list on page 54 for more information on parenting younger adolescents.

Application to life: Help your son or daughter see how values apply to choices in daily life. Look for teachable moments (through television, movies, stories, and so forth) that provide an opportunity to discuss positive choices.

Be sure to recognize and affirm young people when they live out gospel values.

- Which of these suggestions is most helpful to you?
- How can you apply these suggestions in your family?

Putting values into practice

Review what you have learned and complete the Family Coat of Values.

Create a Family Coat of Values. Put your family name at the top. In each of the six sections, write a value plus one or two ways you want your family to live out this value.

Invite each person to share with the group one value and the ways they want to live out this value at home. Encourage others in the group to add ideas.

Family Coat of Values

At home, hold a brief family meeting to share your values and ideas with your son or daughter and invite her or him to add ideas. As a family, commit to living these six values over the next several months. Post your plan on the refrigerator (or other prominent place in the house). Review your success at the end of each month.

A further look

Read aloud the reflection on Baptism. Take time to identify a symbol or image and then share these ideas with the group.

The apostle Paul says, "Let the same mind be in you that was in Christ Jesus…" (Philippians 2:5). In Baptism we promise to guide our children in putting on the mind and heart of Christ. When we adopt and live the values of Jesus we are putting on the mind and heart of Christ.

- Think of a symbol or image for your family that reflects putting on the mind and heart of Christ.

- Take time at home to create or find this symbol and display it in a special place to remind everyone to live the values of Jesus.

Wrap-up

See page 9 in the introduction for a description of "Wrap-up" items. See page 50 for suggested closing prayers.

Before you go, take time for the following:

- Group ministry task

- Review

- Personal concerns and prayer concerns

- Closing prayers

Daily walk

Bible readings

Day 1
Matthew 5:1-12

Day 2
Matthew 5:21-26

Day 3
Matthew 5:38-42

Day 4
Matthew 5:43-48

Day 5
Matthew 7:1-5

Day 6
Matthew 25:31-46

Day 7
Matthew 22:34-40

Verse for the journey

For where your treasure is, there your heart will be also.
Matthew 6:21

Thought for the journey

Values are the internal compasses that guide us as we make decisions and set priorities.

Prayer for the journey

Loving God, help us to teach gospel values to our children. Show us how to live out gospel values and put on the mind and heart of Christ. Amen

3 Celebrating Rituals as a Family

Focus

Rituals are essential for family life. Family rituals give us a sense of permanence and the assurance that even the most ordinary family activities are meaningful and significant.

It would be helpful to have family ritual books available to review during the session. See the list on page 54 for suggestions.

Community building

Recalling family rituals

Reflect on the questions and then share stories.

In this chapter, we will explore the importance of family rituals and identify rituals appropriate to families with younger adolescents.

Recall one significant ritual or celebration that your family observed together, at home or at church, when you were a younger adolescent.

- Was this ritual meaningful to you?
- Did you experience God through this ritual?

Option

Share responses to the following: Recall one experience of worship or ritual celebration in your church that really moved you. How were you moved? Was this worship service or ritual celebration meaningful to you? Did you experience God through this worship service or ritual?

Opening prayer

[1] Make a joyful noise to the Lord, all the earth.
[2] Worship the Lord with gladness;
come into his presence with singing.
[3] Know that the Lord is God.
It is he that made us, and we are his;
we are his people, and the sheep of his pasture.
[4] Enter his gates with thanksgiving,
and his courts with praise.
Give thanks to him, bless his name.
[5] For the Lord is good;
his steadfast love endures forever,
and his faithfulness to all generations.

Psalm 100

The importance of family rituals

Discuss the question and then read the reflection on rituals.

■ Why do you think rituals are so important for healthy family life and for growing in faith as a family?

Family rituals can be extremely simple or more involved. Some rituals occur daily—in the morning, before and after meals, or at bedtime—while others come along weekly, yearly, or once in a lifetime. They can be used to observe special days, such as Christmas and birthdays, as well as the more routine times in family life. Rituals are appropriate during times of celebration as well as loss.

Rituals are important for people of all ages. When we observe rituals that have been handed down through the years or create new ones just for our families, we help our children to live and grow in faith. Rituals provide opportunities for families to slow down and see God's presence in each day, think about the meaning of life's major events and daily happenings, and celebrate God's goodness.

Younger adolescents learn what faith means to them by observing and participating in rituals and celebrations with their parents and the Christian community. This is how faith becomes real for them.

■ What did you learn about the importance of rituals for family life and for growing in faith as a family?

■ What role do the rituals of faith play in your life today? In your family's life?

■ What role would you like rituals of faith to play in your family's life?

Consider this

Rituals can nurture your son or daughter's growth in faith and build up assets for social competencies and positive identity. (See assets 32-40 on pages 52-53.)

■ **Which of these assets could be reinforced as you and your son or daughter participate in rituals?**

■ **Which of these assets would you like to reinforce in your family today?**

Ecclesiastes 3:1-2,4,6-7

Read the Scripture
passage together.

**¹ For everything there is a season, and a time for every matter under heaven:
² a time to be born, and a time to die;
a time to plant, and a time to pluck up what is planted;
⁴ a time to weep, and a time to laugh;
a time to mourn, and a time to dance;
⁶ a time to seek, and a time to lose;
a time to keep, and a time to throw away;
⁷ a time to tear, and a time to sew;
a time to keep silence, and a time to speak.**

Rituals throughout the day and week

Read and discuss.

Rituals throughout the day help us to recognize and celebrate God's daily presence in our family life. Family rituals can grow and adapt to the needs of younger adolescents. New rituals can also be started during this new stage in life.

There are many possibilities for daily or weekly family rituals: prayer in the morning; table blessings (before and after meals); times of thanksgiving, joy or sorrow; times of forgiveness and healing; times of sending forth (leaving for school or work, to a sports game, to summer camp, to volunteering); times of crisis (injury, sickness, loss, disappointments, failures); and times of accomplishment (improved grades, a new job, sports or music achievement).

- What are the possibilities for daily rituals of faith in your family today?

- Which family rituals will you keep or adapt? Which new rituals can you add to your family life?

Locate a one-page
annual calendar and
make a copy for each
person in the group.
Have the copies and
pens or pencils ready to
distribute. Invite parents
to add new ideas to
their ritual calendars
and lists.

On a copy of the annual calendar, circle the dates for rituals you celebrate in your home or congregation (festivals and seasons in the church year, family milestones, ethnic traditions, etc.). Make a list of rituals your family celebrates daily or weekly. As a group, make a list of rituals the congregation celebrates daily, weekly, or monthly.

Rituals throughout the year

The church year begins with the season of Advent, then moves through Christmas, Epiphany, Lent, Easter, and Pentecost. Each season offers opportunities for celebrating rituals at home, for example:

Read and then discuss the questions.

Advent: daily Advent prayers, Advent wreath, Jesse tree, Advent calendars, Las Posadas

Christmas: Blessing the Christmas tree, nativity scene, blessing for the Christmas meal, prayer while sharing Christmas gifts

Lent: Ash Wednesday prayer and simple meal, blessing a home Lenten cross, daily Lenten prayers, Holy Week seder meal, Holy Week Scripture readings

Calendar year events, such as Thanksgiving, Mother's Day, and Father's Day, also offer many opportunities for family rituals.

This would be a good time to display books about family rituals. See page 54 for suggestions.

In addition, there are regular opportunities for celebrating life transitions and milestones. Think about the possibilities for observing these events in your family:

a. birthday and baptism day
b. wedding anniversary
c. beginning and graduating from middle school
d. starting a new job
e. moving
f. blessing of a new home
g. death and funeral of a loved one

Invite parents to add new ideas to their ritual calendars and lists.

Consider the many opportunities for celebrating rituals of faith throughout the year: seasons of the church, calendar seasons, and family transitions/milestones. Identify rituals that are already a part of your family life and new rituals that you would like to incorporate into your year.

■ What are the possibilities for celebrating the seasons of the church year with your son or daughter?

■ What are the possibilities for celebrating calendar year events (Thanksgiving, Mother's/Father's Day)?

■ What are the possibilities for celebrating life transitions and milestones?

■ Which rituals from childhood will you keep or adapt? Which new rituals can you add to your family life?

At home with your son or daughter, develop a calendar of daily, weekly, and yearly rituals and post it on the refrigerator (or other prominent place in the house). Keep a record or scrapbook of your ritual celebrations.

Consider this

Rituals are most meaningful in families when everyone is involved in planning the events. Regardless of age, everyone can play a role in planning and celebrating family rituals. Here are some suggestions for creating your own rituals:

1. Choose an occasion or event together.

2. Check with friends and look at resources to see how others have structured rituals for the same occasion or event. (See the resource list on page 54.)

3. Decide on the components of your celebration:

   Symbols: water, oil, cross, bread or other food, candle

   Words: Scripture readings, poetry or literature, stories, spontaneous and structured prayers (the Lord's Prayer), blessings, prayer petitions

   Environment: artwork, banners, photos, tablecloth, plants

   Music: style, instrumental or sung

   Movement: simple gestures, hugs, blessing signs

4. Plan your celebration to fit your family, not the other way around. Involve each person in at least one part of the preparation and celebration.

5. When you're ready, celebrate as a family.

This process will help turn "ordinary" family life experiences into ritual celebrations that have the potential for becoming religiously significant in your home.

A further look

Set up a prayer table with a large white candle, Bible, bowl of water, and small bowl of olive oil. Light the candle as you begin. Play instrumental music in the background.

In this chapter, we remember baptism through a prayer service. Gather quietly around the prayer table. Have one person read aloud the story of Jesus' baptism (Mark 1:9-11). One by one, have each person dip a finger in the water and make the sign of the cross on their forehead.

When all have done this pray: "May these waters renew the grace of our baptism in each one of us." One by one, have each person dip a finger in the oil and make the sign of the cross on their forehead. As each person does this pray: "May Christ strengthen you with his love and power." Close by reading Psalm 23.

Wrap-up

Before you go, take time for the following:

- Group ministry task

- Review

- Personal concerns and prayer concerns

- Closing prayers

Daily walk

Bible readings

Day 1
Luke 22:7-20

Day 2
Acts 2:37-41

Day 3
Psalm 95:1-7

Day 4
Acts 2:43-47

Day 5
Psalm 63:1-8

Day 6
Psalm 95:1-7

Day 7
Micah 6:6-8

Verse for the journey

O come, let us worship and bow down, let us kneel before the Lord, our Maker! Psalm 95:6

Thought for the journey

"Nurture your rituals and they will provide sustenance to your family all your life. Chances are, your best rituals will outlive you, sending your love into generations to come. Bend yourself to the honest hard work of ritual, and the bountiful crop you harvest will be joy."

(Meg Cox. *The Heart of the Family*.
New York: Random House, 1998, page 339)

Prayer for the journey

Lord, guide us as we celebrate the seasons of faith in our family. Draw us closer to each other and to you as we celebrate your presence throughout our day and throughout our year. Amen

4 Praying as a Family

If possible, have prayer resources for families with younger adolescents available. See the list on page 54.

Focus

Prayer is the very heart of our encounter and relationship with God and must lie at the center of family spirituality.

Community building

Prayer in the family begins with parents. This chapter explores the role of prayer in your life and the life of your family.

- Does your family pray? If so, is prayer part of your everyday life?
- What would you like your family to pray for or pray about?

Option

Take a moment to reflect on your prayer life today and then describe it using a color, a song or hymn, a weather condition, or part of nature (sunset, mountains, ocean).

Opening prayer

1 It is good to give thanks to the Lord,
to sing praises to your name, O Most High;
2 to declare your steadfast love in the morning,
and your faithfulness by night,
3 to the music of the lute and the harp,
to the melody of the lyre.
4 For you, O Lord, have made me glad by your work;
at the works of your hands I sing for joy.

Psalm 92:1-4

Discovery

What is prayer?

Share responses to the
questions.

- How would you define prayer?

- What circumstances or events call you to pray?

- Do you feel closest to God alone, in a church setting, in a group, or in nature?

Romans 8:26-27

Read the Scripture
passage together.

26 ...the Spirit helps us in our weakness; for we do not know how to pray as we ought, but that very Spirit intercedes with sighs too deep for words. 27 And God, who searches the heart, knows what is the mind of the Spirit, because the Spirit intercedes for the saints according to the will of God.

Read and discuss.

In *Prayer—Beginning Conversations with God* (Minneapolis: Augsburg, 1995), Richard Beckmen discusses the experience of prayer:

"Some people think prayer is 'saying a prayer'—speaking a particular intention to God. Prayer, however, can be understood more generally than that. Prayer, in a broad sense, links all aspects of our lives to God. God is present in all of life. We might set aside certain times and places for worship, but God is not absent from any time or any place. It is right and proper to pray at all times and in all places.

"Prayer is the name we give to the experience of being in communication with God wherever we are and whatever we are doing. Prayer is experience because it involves our senses, minds, souls, and spirits. When we pray, we know that this is happening. Prayer is a point of interaction with God.

"Prayer is communication because it involves giving and receiving. It is sharing between two living, personal beings— God and yourself. In all the various forms and methods of prayer, there is something going on between the person of the Christian and the person of God. You are sharing your life: your needs, feelings, concerns, and desires. God is responding with divine presence, consolation, insight, and change" (pages 7-8).

- What might you do to strengthen your own prayer life?

- How might you explain prayer to your son or daughter?

Consider this

One of the assets identified by Search Institute deals with adult role models. Read the description of asset 14 on page 52.

■ How can you be a positive role model for prayer in your family and with your son or daughter?

■ What would you like your son or daughter to learn about prayer from watching you or experiencing prayer times with you?

Discovery

Encouraging younger adolescents to pray

■ How can we help younger adolescents to become praying people?

Read and discuss. This would be a good time to display resources on prayer.

Carolyn Luetjue and Meg Marcrander offer the following suggestions on teaching adolescents to pray (*Face to Face with God in Your Home: Guiding Children and Youth in Prayer,* Minneapolis: Augsburg Fortress, 1995):

"Teach your teenagers that there are many ways to pray. We can pray formally, kneeling with eyes closed and hands folded. We can also pray while jogging, delivering newspapers, or studying for a math test. Our prayers can include words of sorrow and pain, expressions of joy and thankfulness, or confessions of guilt and unworthiness. Help your adolescent understand that prayer is simply a conversation with a loving, forgiving, and understanding friend. Our friend Jesus promises to be there always to listen to and answer our prayers" (page 81).

Here are several specific ways to encourage your son or daughter to pray:

> **Discover how and when Jesus prayed:**
> a. Read about Jesus' teachings on prayer: Luke 11:1-13 and Matthew 6:5-15, 7:7-11; Luke 10:21-22; Matthew 11:25-30.
> b. Read about times when Jesus prayed: Mark 1:32-39, Luke 5:15-16, Luke 6:12-13, Luke 9:18-20, Luke 22:39-46 or Matthew 26:35-46 or Mark 14:32-42; Matthew 14:22-23 or Mark 6:45-46, John 17.

Experience and utilize a variety of prayer forms:
a. *Prayers of praise* in which we give praise to God for the mystery and majesty of God.
b. *Prayers of thanksgiving* in which we give thanks for all our blessings in life.
c. *Spontaneous prayers* in which we offer God what is in our hearts and minds.
d. *Prayers of petition* in which we tell God about what we need and what others need.
e. *Prayers of contrition* in which we ask God for forgiveness and healing for our wrongdoing.

Commit to finding a few moments to quietly spend with one another in prayer: In the midst of your busy lives, set aside a regular time for your family to pray.

Keep a prayer concerns list: Place a wipe-off board in a place where everyone in the family can see it and write down prayer concerns for problems, situations, and people. Invite all family members to pray for these prayer concerns.

Use a prayer journal: Give your son or daughter a prayer journal for recording their prayers and reflections. They could also include favorite prayers or Scripture passages, photos and artwork, prayer requests, and personal thoughts.

Pray with Scripture: Recommend Scripture passages that address the concerns and experiences of young people and use these passages in prayer. Here are several suggestions from Psalms:
a. Psalm 8:1-7 (human dignity)
b. Psalm 23:1-6 and Psalm 62:1-12 (trust in God)
c. Psalm 16:1-11 and 139:1-12 (Lord's presence)
d. Psalm 25:1-12 and 32:1-11 (forgiveness)
e. Psalm 30:1-12 (thanksgiving)
f. Psalm 63:1-8 (longing for God)
g. Psalm 86:1-13 (distress)
h. Psalm 103:1-14 (praise of God)
i. Psalm 121:1-8 (help)

Pray about decisions: A helpful tool for solving emotionally-charged issues is to pray about these situations before decisions actually need to be made, allowing the young person to place the decision before God and seek guidance. Recommend Bible passages that speak to the situation, provide helpful insights, and encourage your son or daughter to think about what Jesus would do if confronted with the situation.

Above all, we as parents need to be praying people. Our faith journeys and prayer lives are the most valuable gifts we can give young people!

- Which of these suggestions would you like to use to encourage your son or daughter to pray?

- How can you put these suggestions into practice?

Reflecting on faith in daily life

If time allows, practice this prayer form as a group.

Parents and younger adolescents can look at the world through the eyes of faith by practicing faith reflection in their daily lives. This is not difficult; some of us do it instinctively. It involves turning prayer time into a time of seeing and hearing God's presence in our daily lives and considering the significance and implications which this holds for us as disciples. Faith reflection helps us discover God's presence in our experiences, what difference God's presence makes, and what God expects. This reflection helps us look at an experience in light of our religious beliefs and helps focus our lives according to our beliefs. It is a simple but effective way to teach young people to develop their inner spiritual lives.

Practice the process together with your young person and then encourage your son or daughter to use this as part of their personal prayer time.

1. *Select an experience.* Each day of family life is filled with hundreds of interactions—acts of love, service, compassion, forgiveness. How can we discover God's presence in our daily lives? In each day, look for "firsts" and "lasts" involving transitions (and sometimes crises) that can connect us or drive us apart from each other and God. Also look for moments of new learning and important encounters with a special person or place.

2. *Describe the experience.* In describing the experience, we need to know who was involved. What happened? Where did the event take place? When? How?

3. *Enter the experience.* To enter the experience, close your eyes and try to relive it in your mind. First relive it by identifying your feelings, thoughts, and actions at the time of the experience. Then, relive it by seeing the experience in your mind as if it were being played on a movie screen and you are just observing. Then identify your present feelings and thoughts.

4. *Learn from the experience.* After reliving the experience, ask yourself how you see God present in this. Try to relate the experience to a particular Scripture passage, Christian belief, tradition, or church teaching. Does the experience illustrate God's love for you? Is it an example of being one in Christ's body or an example of Christ's resurrection in today's world? Why is it important to you? What have you learned?

A further look

Read aloud, pray the contemporary adaptation of the Lord's Prayer together, and then discuss the questions.

Baptism immerses us into a life with God who is trinity: God is our parent and provider; Jesus is our redeemer and friend; the Holy Spirit is our sanctifier and consolation. The Lord's Prayer relates us to this life and reminds us who we are and what our Christian lives are all about.

Pray the following contemporary adaptation of the Lord's Prayer.

> Abba in heaven,
> your name is holy!
> Your justice come,
> your will be done,
> on earth as in the heavens.
> Fill us this day
> with all that we need.
> Teach us to heal
> as you have healed us.
> Bring us not to the test,
> but deliver us always
> from the power of evil.
> You alone are God,
> and all belongs to you!

(Edward F. Gabriele. *Gathered at the Table in Prayer and Song.* Winona, MN: St. Mary's Press, 2000, page 25.)

■ What does the Lord's Prayer reveal to us about ourselves?

■ What does the Lord's Prayer reveal to us about prayer and the Christian life?

Wrap-up

Before you go, take time for the following:

- Group ministry task

- Review

- Personal concerns and prayer concerns

- Closing prayers

Daily walk

Bible readings

Day 1
Psalm 148

Day 2
Psalm 116

Day 3
Psalm 95:1-7

Day 4
Psalm 71

Day 5
Psalm 20

Day 6
Psalm 111

Day 7
Psalm 143

Verse for the journey

Ask, and it will be given you; search, and you will find; knock, and the door will be opened for you. For everyone who asks receives, and everyone who searches finds, and for everyone who knocks, the door will be opened. Matthew 7:7-8

Thought for the journey

"Prayer is the name we give to the experience of being in communication with God, wherever we are and whatever we are doing."

(Richard Beckmen, *Prayer—Beginning Conversations with God*,
Minneapolis: Augsburg, 1995, page 8)

Prayer for the journey

Lord,
Make me an instrument of your peace.
Where there is hatred, let me sow love;
Where there is injury, pardon;
Where there is doubt, faith;
Where there is despair, hope;
Where there is darkness, light;
Where there is sadness, joy.

(Francis of Assisi, 1182-1226)

5 Serving as a Family

It would be helpful to have service books available to review. See the list on page 54 for suggestions. It would also be helpful to have a list of church and community service projects for families with young people.

Focus

The calls to serve and work for justice are central themes in the Bible. When families serve the needs of others, they follow in the footsteps of Jesus and grow in faith as a family.

Community building

Using the letters in the word "JUSTICE," describe what the justice means to you. ("J," for example, may recall the fact that our Christian understanding of justice flows from the life and ministry of Jesus; "U," on the other hand, may point to a concrete justice concern like unemployment.)

J _____

U _____

S _____

T _____

I _____

C _____

E _____

Option

Complete the following unfinished sentences.

■ **A social problem I wish we could fix...**

■ **The world would be a better place if...**

■ **A person who embodies a life of justice and service is...**

■ **It is important for Christians to serve others because...**

Opening prayer

Lord, teach us what it means to be "poor in spirit" in a consumer society; to comfort those who suffer in our midst; to "show mercy" in an often unforgiving world; to "hunger and thirst for justice" in a nation still challenged by hunger and homelessness, poverty and prejudice; and to be "peacemakers" in an often violent and fearful world. Amen

The call to justice and service

Have one person read Psalm 146 and another read Matthew 25. Then discuss the questions.

Our Christian faith calls us to work for justice; to serve those in need; to pursue peace; and to defend the life, dignity, and rights of all our sisters and brothers.

Psalm 146:5-9

5 **Happy are those whose help is the God of Jacob,**
whose hope is in the Lord their God,
6 **who made heaven and earth,**
the sea, and all that is in them;
who keeps faith forever;
7 **who executes justice for the oppressed;**
who gives food to the hungry.
The Lord sets the prisoners free;
8 **the Lord opens the eyes of the blind.**
The Lord lifts up those who are bowed down;
the Lord loves the righteous.
9 **The Lord watches over the strangers;**
he upholds the orphan and the widow,
but the way of the wicked he brings to ruin.

Matthew 25:34-40

34 **Then the king will say to those at his right hand, 'Come, you that are blessed by my Father, inherit the kingdom prepared for you from the foundation of the world;** 35 **for I was hungry and you gave me food, I was thirsty and you gave me something to drink, I was a stranger and you welcomed me,** 36 **I was naked and you gave me clothing, I was sick and you took care of me, I was in prison and you visited me.'** 37 **Then the righteous will answer him, 'Lord, when was it that we saw you hungry and gave you food, or thirsty and gave you something to drink?** 38 **And when was it that we saw you a stranger and welcomed you, or naked and gave you clothing?** 39 **And when was it that we saw you sick or in prison and visited you?'** 40 **And the king will answer them, 'Truly I tell you, just as you did it to one of the least of these who are members of my family, you did it to me.'**

- What do these passages say to you about the importance of justice and service in the Christian faith?

- What are the implications of the Lord God defending the oppressed (Psalm 146) and of Jesus identifying himself with those in need (Matthew 25)?

■ Imagine what the world would be like if the message embodied in these Bible passages became a reality in our time. What would it mean for your life, your family's life, your community, and our nation and world?

Review the benefits of service and assets 9, 26, and 27. Then discuss the questions.

Consider this

According to Search Institute's overall work and research, involvement in service provides numerous benefits to adolescents and parents alike:

a. Serving helps make the Christian faith real.
b. Serving promotes healthy lifestyles and choices.
c. Serving helps to develop positive self-esteem, self-confidence, and social skills.
d. Serving helps people discover their personal gifts and abilities and increases self-esteem and moral reasoning abilities.
e. Serving teaches new skills and perspectives.
f. Serving nurtures a lifelong commitment to service and justice involvement.
g. Serving builds a stronger sense of community within the family and among families who serve.
h. Serving has an impact on people who are served. Their needs are met, and they receive a sense of hope and empowerment.
i. Serving improves the quality of life and the climate of the community.

Three of the 40 assets for healthy development explicitly focus on the importance of the service: #9 (service to others (family values caring), and #27 (family values equality and social justice). Read about these on pages 52-53.

■ What do you see as the benefits of family service? Which benefits seem most important or significant to you?

■ How can involvement in service benefit you and your son or daughter?

Read and discuss.

Living justice and service

As we grow in our faith, we become more aware of how central God's justice was to Jesus' life and ministry. As parents of younger adolescents, this dimension of faith can be incorporated into our parenting and family life in a variety of ways.

Actions of direct service are a logical starting point for families with younger adolescents. These young people easily connect with direct service and the needs that prompt it. Being involved with service projects allows them to give of themselves and to see the results of their efforts. As parents, it is important to assist our sons and daughters in connecting acts of service with our Christian faith. Younger adolescents need to know that they are important and that God can use them right now.

Our efforts to feed the hungry, shelter the homeless, welcome the stranger, and serve the poor and vulnerable must be accompanied by works of justice—concrete efforts to address the causes of human suffering and injustice. It is important to assist our sons and daughters in understanding the need to change those situations that make people victims of injustice in the first place. Participating in struggles for social change can give hope to younger adolescents if the issues are concrete enough or have a direct bearing on them. For example, families working at a homeless shelter or soup kitchen could also be involved with a local coalition for the homeless that is working to create housing, employment, and just policies for the homeless. In this way, families experience the benefits of working directly with the homeless and learn to change the system which keeps people homeless.

Families with younger adolescents can put their faith into practice through works of justice and service by:

a. promoting positive ways to resolve conflict within the family and the community

b. standing in opposition to the violence that permeates our culture and world

c. learning about and discussing important social issues; learning more about the Bible's teachings on justice, peace, and service

d. caring for the earth and its resources

e. living simply and taking good care of personal and family possessions

f. praying regularly for greater justice and peace, and for those in need

g. sharing family time, talents, and possessions with people in need

h. participating in church or community service projects as a family

i. dedicating a week of family vacation time to a service program such as Habitat for Humanity

j. making financial donations to support the efforts of local and national groups who work directly with the poor or work for justice on behalf of the poor

k. advocating for public policies that promote dignity, preserve God's creation, and build peace

l. joining with other families to work for greater charity, justice, and peace

Consider adopting a service project each month or season.

■ Are you and your family already involved in service in your church and community?

■ How is your congregation engaged in justice and service?

■ What organizations in your community are engaged in justice and service? Who do they serve?

■ How can your family become involved in justice and service, locally and globally?

A further look

Have someone read this section aloud, then share ideas for the pledge within the large group.

A family commitment to serve

Baptism empowers us for our mission as Christians. For all who follow Jesus, serving the needs of others and working for justice are essential.

It has been said that no one can do everything, but everyone can do something. Each of us has unique abilities, a certain amount of time, and financial resources. Are there changes that you can make in allocating your talent, time, and treasure so that you can serve those in need and promote the work of justice—locally, nationally, globally?

With your son or daughter, reaffirm your baptismal mission by writing a family pledge for justice and service.

A Pledge

This is what God asks of you, and only this: That you act justly, love tenderly, and walk humbly with your God
Micah 6:8

In the attempt to act justly and serve those in need, our family will…

Wrap-up

Before you go, take time for the following:

- **Group ministry task**

- **Review**

- **Personal concerns and prayer concerns**

- **Closing prayers**

Daily walk

Bible readings

Day 1
Deuteronomy 30:15-20

Day 2
Isaiah 2:1-5

Day 3
Isaiah 61:1-2

Day 4
Psalm 146

Day 5
Luke 3:10-14

Day 6
Acts 4:32-35

Day 7
1 John 4:19-21

Verse for the journey

This is what God asks of you, and only this: That you act justly, love tenderly, and walk humbly with your God. Micah 6:8

Thought for the journey

Younger adolescents need to know that they are important and that God can use them right now.

Prayer for the journey

God, true light and source of all light, may we recognize you in oppressed people and poor people, in homeless people and hungry people. May we be a means of healing, strength, and peace by using our gifts in the service of others. We ask this in the name of Jesus, your son. Amen

6 Relating as a Family

It would be helpful to have parenting and family enrichment books available to review. See the list on page 54 for suggestions.

Effective parenting and a strong home life evolve from the commitment to build upon your family's strengths and to develop the skills necessary for families with younger adolescents.

Community building

Allow time for everyone to reflect, then share responses.

■ One of my greatest gifts or strengths as a parent of a younger adolescent is…

■ Tell a brief story that illustrates one of your parenting gifts or strengths.

Option

Describe your family life using a TV commercial; a TV show, Broadway musical or feature film; a popular song; or a book title.

Opening prayer

Gracious God, give us the strength and wisdom to build our families on the foundations of love and compassion, kindness and generosity, humility and gentleness, forgiveness and peace. Amen

Qualities of a faithful family

Discuss the question
and have one person
read the Scripture pas-
sage aloud.

■ Take a moment to think about the qualities you would like to see in your family. How would you like to be able to describe your life as a family?

Colossians 3:12-17

12 As God's chosen ones, holy and beloved, clothe yourselves with compassion, kindness, humility, meekness, and patience. 13 Bear with one another and, if anyone has a complaint against another, forgive each other; just as the Lord has forgiven you, so you also must forgive. 14 Above all, clothe yourselves with love, which binds everything together in perfect harmony. 15 And let the peace of Christ rule in your hearts, to which indeed you were called in the one body. And be thankful. 16 Let the word of Christ dwell in you richly; teach and admonish one another in all wisdom; and with gratitude in your hearts sing psalms, hymns, and spiritual songs to God. 17 And whatever you do, in word or deed, do everything in the name of the Lord Jesus, giving thanks to God the Father through him.

Paul's letter to the Colossians describes the essential qualities of a Christian family as well as the Christian community.

■ What would it be like if you lived this vision in your family?

Building on your strengths

Read the eight qualities
and discuss the
questions.

Two researchers, Nick Stinnett and John DeFrain, interviewed thousands of families and identified eight qualities of strong families. They found that all families have strengths, and families become stronger by discovering and developing their particular strengths. Strong families are not problem-free, but rather have learned to harness their resources to surmount difficulties.

A strong family…

    a. shares a sense of commitment and connectedness.

    b. spends both quality and quantity time together sharing many areas of life.

    c. engages in communication that is clear, open, frequent, and honest.

    d. appreciates each person. Members take time to let one another know this in a variety of ways.

    e. has clearly defined roles for family members.

    f. has a shared religious and moral core.

    g. is involved in the community.

    h. is able to cope with crises and times of stress in a positive manner.

■ Which qualities of strong families do you find in your family today?

■ Which qualities do you want to build up in your family? How will you do this?

Consider this

Many of the 40 assets from Search Institute describe skills that are necessary for effective family life and for the healthy growth of adolescents. To explore their importance, read about assets 1, 2, 11, 32, 33, 35, 36, 37, 38, 39 and 40 on pages 52-53.

■ **How important are these assets for nurturing the positive growth of younger adolescents?**

■ **How can you strengthen these assets in your family? What concrete actions can you take to promote these assets in your son or daughter?**

Communicating with younger adolescents

Review suggestions and discuss the questions.

One of the keys to a strong family is communication that is clear, open, frequent, and honest. Parents and younger adolescents sometimes find it difficult to connect with each other's thoughts and feelings, even when they make time for each other. Here are several suggestions for improving the communication between you and your son or daughter:

First, spend time with each other. If parents and younger adolescents spend time together regularly, the tough topics are a bit easier to handle.

Second, recognize and reduce roadblocks to effective communication. Several of the most common obstacles to communication are lack of time; normal adolescent changes such as self-consciousness, limited verbal skills, the growing need for some independence, and increased resistance to authority; inappropriate and ineffective methods of communicating that occur when parents belittle the importance of an issue, criticize or ridicule, judge or blame, give too many orders or too much advice, offer solutions before the issues have been discussed adequately, threaten, and/or preach.

Third, seek first to understand, and then to be understood. Most people do not listen with the intent to understand; they listen with the intent to reply. They are either speaking or preparing to speak. Listen to your son or daughter with the intent to understand—listen with your ears but also listen with your eyes and with your heart. Communication is truly effective when there is a balance between the desires to understand others and to be understood by them.

Fourth, understand and accept where your son or daughter is at developmentally. It is natural for younger adolescents to be preoccupied with themselves as they experience tremendous amounts of change, so be very careful about giving negative feedback. Simply asking a "feeling" question, such as "How do you feel about..." may open new dimensions in conversation.

Finally, focus on the concerns and interests of your son or daughter. Younger adolescents may not have the courage or the know-how to initiate conversation about their personal concerns and worries, so parents may need to take the lead in opening up a variety of topics.

In addition, a general question or comment in any one of the following areas may lead to a good conversation:

Family matters: decisions and issues that affect your son or daughter and the whole family

Controversial issues: sexuality, drugs and alcohol, etc.

The Big Whys: Why do people go to war? Why does God let people go hungry? Why does God allow suffering?

The future: jobs, careers, technical school/college

Current events: news, issues, and problems in the community, nation, and world

Personal interests and concerns of young people: activities such as sports, hobbies, friends, and school, and concerns about their looks, school performance, or losing a parent or best friend

Parents and family history: stories that reveal your emotional side and human frailties as well as stories about your adolescent years; and stories about the family's history, grandparents and relatives, or family traditions

Think about the way you and your son or daughter communicate and then answer these questions:

- How has the frequency of communication with your son or daughter changed over the years? Have these changes been positive or negative?

- What do you talk about? What would you like to spend more time talking about?

- What keeps you and your son or daughter from communicating? What can you do about this?

- What is one thing you would change about the way you and your son or daughter talk with each other?

A further look

In Baptism we are given a new birth by water and the Holy Spirit. In the letter to the Galatians, Paul challenges us to live in the Spirit. As Paul writes, "the fruit of the Spirit is love, joy, peace, patience, kindness, generosity, faithfulness, gentleness, and self-control" (Galatians 5:22-23).

- ■ How has the Holy Spirit blessed your family with these fruits or qualities?

- ■ Take a moment for prayer. Reflect on which of these fruits your family most needs now. Pray to the Holy Spirit to respond to your need.

Wrap-up

Before you go, take time for the following:

- Group ministry task

- Review

- Personal concerns and prayer concerns

- Closing prayers

Daily walk

Bible readings

Day 1
Romans 12:9-13

Day 2
John 15:12-17

Day 3
1 Corinthians 13:1-13

Day 4
Luke 6:37-39

Day 5
Philippians 2:1-11

Day 6
Ephesians 4:1-6

Day 7
Deuteronomy 6:1-9

Verse for the journey

Love is patient; love is kind; love is not envious or boastful or arrogant or rude. It does not insist on its own way; it is not irritable or resentful; it does not rejoice in wrongdoing, but rejoices in the truth. It bears all things, believes all things, hopes all things, endures all things. 1 Corinthians 13:4-7

Thought for the journey

One of the keys to a strong family is communication that is clear, open, frequent, and honest.

Prayer for the journey

Gracious God, thank you for our families. Teach us to maintain clear, open, frequent, and honest communication with our sons and daughters. Help our families to live and grow in faith each day. Amen

Appendix

Group directory

Record information about group members here.

Names	Addresses	Phone numbers

Prayers

■ Closing Prayer

Lord God, you have called your servants to ventures of which we cannot see the ending, by paths as yet untrodden, through perils unknown. Give us faith to go out with good courage, not knowing where we go, but only that your hand is leading us and your love supporting us; through Jesus Christ our Lord. Amen

From *Lutheran Book of Worship* (page 153) copyright © 1978.

(If you plan to pray the Lord's Prayer, record the version your group uses in the next column.)

■ The Lord's Prayer

Group commitments

Do not be conformed to this world, but be transformed by the renewing of your minds, so that you may discern what is the will of God—what is good and acceptable and perfect. Romans 12:2.

■ For our time together, we have made the following commitments to each other

■ Goals for our study of this topic are

■ Our group ministry task is

■ My personal action plan is

Prayer requests

40 Developmental Assets for Adolescents

EXTERNAL ASSETS

ASSET TYPE	ASSET NAME	ASSET DEFINITION
Support	1. Family support	Family life provides high levels of love and support.
	2. Positive family communication	Young person and her or his parent(s) communicate positively, and young person is willing to seek advice and counsel from parent(s).
	3. Other adult relationships	Young person receives support from three or more nonparent adults.
	4. Caring neighborhood	Young person experiences caring neighbors.
	5. Caring school climate	School provides a caring, encouraging environment.
	6. Parent involvement in schooling	Parent(s) are actively involved in helping young person succeed in school.
Empowerment	7. Community values youth	Young person perceives that adults in the community value youth.
	8. Youth as resources	Young people are given useful roles in the community.
	9. Service to others	Young person serves in the community one hour or more per week.
	10. Safety	Young person feels safe at home, at school, and in the neighborhood.
Boundaries and Expectations	11. Family boundaries	Family has clear rules and consequences, and monitors the young person's whereabouts.
	12. School boundaries	School provides clear rules and consequences.
	13. Neighborhood boundaries	Neighbors take responsibility for monitoring young people's behavior.
	14. Adult role models	Parent(s) and other adults model positive, responsible behavior.
	15. Positive peer influence	Young person's best friends model responsible behavior.
	16. High expectations	Both parent(s) and teachers encourage the young person to do well.
Constructive Use of Time	17. Creative activities	Young person spends three or more hours per week in lessons or practice in music, theater, or other arts.
	18. Youth programs	Young person spends three or more hours per week in sports, clubs, or organizations at school and/or in community organizations.
	19. Religious community	Young person spends one hour or more per week in activities in a religious institution.
	20. Time at home	Young person is out with friends "with nothing special to do" two or fewer nights per week.

INTERNAL ASSETS

ASSET TYPE	ASSET NAME	ASSET DEFINITION
Commitment to Learning	21. Achievement motivation	Young person is motivated to do well in school.
	22. School engagement	Young person is actively engaged in learning.
	23. Homework	Young person reports doing at least one hour of homework every school day.
	24. Bonding to school	Young person cares about her or his school.
	25. Reading for pleasure	Young person reads for pleasure three or more hours per week.
Positive Values	26. Caring	Young person places high value on helping other people.
	27. Equality and social justice	Young person places high value on promoting equality and reducing hunger and poverty.
	28. Integrity	Young person acts on convictions and stands up for her or his beliefs.
	29. Honesty	Young person "tells the truth even when it is not easy."
	30. Responsibility	Young person accepts and takes personal responsibility.
	31. Restraint	Young person believes it is important not to be sexually active or to use alcohol or other drugs.
Social Competencies	32. Planning and decision making	Young person knows how to plan ahead and make choices.
	33. Interpersonal competence	Young person has empathy, sensitivity, and friendship skills.
	34. Cultural competence	Young person has knowledge of and comfort with people of different cultural/racial/ethnic backgrounds.
	35. Resistance skills	Young person can resist negative peer pressure and dangerous situations.
	36. Peaceful conflict resolution	Young person seeks to resolve conflict nonviolently.
Positive Identity	37. Personal power	Young person feels he or she has control over "things that happen to me."
	38. Self-esteem	Young person reports having a high self-esteem.
	39. Sense of purpose	Young person reports that "my life has a purpose."
	40. Positive view of personal future	Young person is optimistic about her or his personal future.

Resources

Alberswerth, Deborah and Laura Loving. *Celebrating at Home: Prayers and Liturgies for Families.* Cleveland, Ohio: United Church Press, 1998.

Beckmen, Richard. *Prayer: Beginning Conversations with God.* Minneapolis: Augsburg Fortress, 1995.

Benson, Peter, Judy Galbraith and Pamela Espeland. *What Kids Need to Succeed.* Minneapolis: Free Spirit Publishing, 1998.

Chesto, Kathleen. *Family Prayer for Family Times—Traditions, Celebrations, and Rituals.* Mystic, CT: Twenty-third Publications, 1996.

Covey, Stephen. *The Seven Habits of Highly Effective Families.* New York: Golden Books, 1997.

DeGrote-Sorensen, Barbara and David Sorensen. *Escaping the Family Time Trap: Workbook for Over Busy Families.* Minneapolis: Augsburg Books, 2001.

Dosick, Wayne. *Golden Rules—The Ten Ethical Values Parents Need to Teach Their Children.* San Francisco: HarperSanFrancisco, 1995.

Eittreim, Jean Brown. *That Reminds Me: Family Story-Starters for Passing on the Faith.* Minneapolis: Augsburg Books, 1998.

Eyre, Linda and Richard. *Teaching Your Children Values.* New York: Fireside, 1993.

Finley, Mitch and Kathy. *Building Christian Families.* Allen, TX: Thomas More/Tabor, 1996.

Kallestad, Walter. *The Everyday Anytime Guide to Prayer.* Minneapolis: Augsburg Books, 1995.

Luetje, Carolyn and Meg Marcrander. *Face to Face with God in Your Home: Guiding Children and Youth in Prayer.* Minneapolis: Augsburg Fortress, 1995.

McCarty, Robert. *Tips for Raising Teens—A Primer for Parents.* New York: Paulist Press, 1998.

McGinnis, James, Ken and Gretchen Lovingood, and Jim Vogt. *Families Creating a Circle of Peace.* St. Louis: Families Against Violence Advocacy Network/Institute for Peace and Justice, 1996.

McGrath, Tom. *Raising Faith-Filled Kids.* Chicago: Loyola Press, 2000.

Nelson, Gertrude Mueller. *To Dance with God—Family Ritual and Community Celebration.* New York: Paulist Press, 1986.

O'Neal, Debbie Trafton. *The Family Hand-Me-Down Book: Ways to Build and Preserve History.* Minneapolis: Augsburg Books, 2000.

Payden, Deborah Alberswerth and Laura Loving. *Celebrating at Home-Prayers and Liturgies for Families.* Cleveland: United Church Press, 1998.

Saso, Patt and Steve. *10 Best Gifts for Your Teen.* Notre Dame, IN: Ave Maria Press, 1999.

Seo, Danny. *Heaven on Earth—15 Minute Miracles to Change the World.* New York: Pocket Books, 1999.

Stinnett, Nick, and Michael O'Donnell. *Good Kids—How You and Your Kids Can Successfully Navigate the Teen Years.* New York: Doubleday, 1996.

Thompson, Marjorie. *Family—The Forming Center.* Nashville: Upper Room Books, 1996.

Young, Peter. *Celebrate Life—Rituals for Home and Church.* Cleveland: United Church Press, 1999.

See the Center for Ministry Development's website at http://cmdnet.org for more resources for parents and children.

See the Search Institute's website at http://www.search-institute.org for more information on the 40 developmental assets for growth.

Please tell us about your experience with INTERSECTIONS.

4. What I like best about my INTERSECTIONS experience is

5. Three things I want to see the same in future INTERSECTIONS books are

6. Three things I might change in future INTERSECTIONS books are

7. Topics I would like developed for new INTERSECTIONS books are

8. Our group had _____ sessions for the six chapters of this book.

9. Other comments I have about INTERSECTIONS are

Thank you for taking the time to fill out and return this questionnaire.

----------------------- FOLD CARD IN HERE, SEAL WITH TAPE, AND MAIL TODAY! -----------------------

Name _____

Address _____

Daytime telephone _____

Please check the INTERSECTIONS book you are evaluating.

- [ ] The Bible and Life
- [ ] Caring and Community
- [ ] Death and Grief
- [ ] Faith
- [ ] Following Jesus
- [ ] Integrity
- [ ] Jesus: Divine and Human
- [ ] Managing Stress
- [ ] Parenting
- [ ] Parenting: Raising Faithful Preschoolers
- [ ] Parenting: Raising Faithful Grade-schoolers
- [ ] Parenting: Raising Faithful Younger Adolescents
- [ ] Parenting: Raising Faithful Older Adolescents
- [ ] Peace
- [ ] Praying
- [ ] Reconcilable Differences
- [ ] Smart Choices

Please tell us about your small group.

1. Our group had an average attendance of _____ .

2. Our group was made up of
   _____ Young adults (19-25 years).
   _____ Adults (most between 25-45 years).
   _____ Adults (most between 45-60 years).
   _____ Adults (most between 60-75 years).
   _____ Adults (most 75 and over).
   _____ Adults (wide mix of ages).
   _____ Men (number) and _____ women (number).

3. Our group (answer as many as apply)
   _____ came together for the sole purpose of studying this INTERSECTIONS book.
   _____ has decided to study another INTERSECTIONS book.
   _____ is an ongoing Sunday school group.
   _____ met at a time other than Sunday morning.
   _____ had only one facilitator for this study.

NO POSTAGE
NECESSARY
IF MAILED
IN THE
UNITED STATE

BUSINESS REPLY MAIL

FIRST-CLASS MAIL   PERMIT NO. 22120   MINNEAPOLIS, MN

POSTAGE WILL BE PAID BY ADDRESSEE

Augsburg Fortress

ATTN INTERSECTIONS TEAM
PO BOX 1209
MINNEAPOLIS MN 55440-8807